Ten Poems about Knitting

ex libris

Candlestick Press

Published by:
Candlestick Press,
Diversity House, 72 Nottingham Road,
Arnold, Nottingham NG5 6LF
www.candlestickpress.co.uk

Printed by Ratcliff & Roper Print Group, Nottinghamshire, UK

Introduction © Di Slaney, 2015

Illustrations, including cover © Jan Brewerton, 2015
www.janbrewerton.co.uk

ISBN 978 1 907598 29 6

Dedicated to the memory of Doris Conroy (1907 – 1983)

Acknowledgements:
Our thanks to our friends Alison Binks and Sarah Doherty of Yarn in
Beeston (www.yarn-in-notts.co.uk) for knitting input and to Lorraine
Mariner for poetry research. Thanks to Roy Fisher for permission to
reprint 'Neighbours We'll Not Part Tonight' (1957), first published
by Circle Press (1976). Our thanks also to Christopher James for
permission to reprint 'The Manly Art of Knitting', which appeared
in his collection of the same name, published by Templar Poetry
(2011). Lydia Towsey's poem, 'Wool', first appeared in *Magma 59*
and is printed here by kind permission of the author. 'The Symbolism
of Ancient Sweaters' from 'How to Knit a Poem' by Gwyneth Lewis
is reprinted from *Sparrow Tree*, Bloodaxe Books (2011) and Jackie
Kay, 'The Knitter', first appeared in *Darling: New and Selected Poems*,
Bloodaxe Books (2007). Sue Dymoke, 'Janet's', first appeared in *The
New Girls*, Shoestring Press (2004) and is reprinted by kind permission
of the author. 'Dropped Stitches' by Jane Duran was first published in
Graceline, Enitharmon Press (2010); Allison McVety, 'Needle Work'
first appeared in *The Night Trotsky Came to Stay*, Smith/Doorstop
Books (2007). 'For My Grandmother Knitting' by Liz Lochhead was
first published in *Dreaming Frankenstein & Collected Poems 1967 –
1984*, Polygon Books, 1984.

Where poets are no longer living, their dates are given.

Introduction

As a child, one of my earliest memories is of sitting in an empty
yarn box hearing the knitting machines and overlockers at work
in my Nana's knitting factory in Nottingham's Lace Market.
I didn't know then that we were part of a 400-year tradition
of textile industry in Nottinghamshire and the East Midlands.
Machine knitting was invented in 1589 by William Lee from
Calverton, to win the heart of a woman who preferred to knit her
own stockings rather than go courting with him, if local folklore
is to be believed.

I can still smell that unique combination of dust, wool and burnt
toast, the scent of every Saturday morning in the factory. As a
consequence, our family had a wide selection of jumpers for
every occasion – summer holiday snaps always have us wearing
cardigans and heading for craft and wool shops, some kind of
genetic imprinting drawing us to the known source of comfort,
warmth and protection.

Now I have my own sheep, with my first batch of wool
processed to yarn for knitting up by people far more proficient
than I with a pair of needles. I like the idea of yarn representing
the tale – the poems – in this pamphlet, words knitted together
by expert craftspeople. And I love the fact that we have several
local writers featured here, carrying on established Midlands'
traditions in words and wool - from Lydia Towsey's unravelling
relationship in 'Wool' to Jessie Pope's soldier-supporting army
of sock knitters in 'The Knitting Song', and Sue Dymoke's
wonderful 'hushed world' of the wool shop in 'Janet's'.

Knitting as a metaphor for life is beautifully and poignantly
described in Jackie Kay's 'The Knitter', knitting not only to
'keep death away' but also to 'hold a good yarn'. We hope you
enjoy reading the ten good yarns in this pamphlet as much as we
have enjoyed casting them on.

Di Slaney

The Symbolism of Ancient Sweaters

Homemade sweaters contain a code
To be read by initiates. This bobbling here's
A marriage proposal, the Fair-Isle cuff
Says: 'The dog is a spy. Meet me in town
On Tuesday.' Even more arcane
Are garments made by knitting machine.
I once had a sweater that must have declared:
'I only like men with facial hair.' They came.
The way you knit is how you make love,
How you are with your God.
It's a question of soul, of daily repair.
If space is made of superstrings,
Then God's a knitter, everything
Is craft, and perhaps we could darn
Tears in the space-time continuum.

Gwyneth Lewis

The Knitter

I knit to keep death away
for home will dae me.
On a day like this the fine mist
is a dropped stitch across the sky.

I knit to hold a good yarn
for stories bide with me
on a night like this, by the peat fire;
I like a story with a herringbone twist.

But a yarn aye slips through your fingers.
And my small heart has shrunk with years.
I couldn't measure the gravits, the gloves, the mittens,
the jerseys, the cuffs, the hose, the caps,

the cowls, the cravats, the cardigans,
the hems and facings over the years.
Beyond the sea wall, the waves unfurl.
I knitted through the wee stitched hours.

I knitted till my eyes filled with tears,
till the dark sky filled with colour.
Every spare moment. Time was a ball of wool.
I knitted to keep my croft; knitted to save my life.

When my man was out at sea; I knitted the fishbone.
Three to the door, three to the fire.
The more I could knit; the more we could eat.
I knitted to mend my broken heart

when the sea took my man away, and by day
I knitted to keep the memories at bay.
I knitted my borders by the light of the fire
when the full moon in the sky was a fresh ball of yarn.

I knitted to begin again: Lay on, sweerie geng.
Takkin my makkin everywhere I gang.
Een and een. Twin pins. My good head.
A whole life of casting on, casting off

like the North sea. I watch wave after wave,
plain and purl, casting on, casting off.
I watch the ferries coming back, going away.
Time is a loop stitch. I knit to keep death away.

Jackie Kay

The Manly Art of Knitting

When my father taught us to knit
he held the needles like fencing swords,
told us how Cary Grant never dropped
a stitch in *Mr Lucky*; we listened
to the clack of his pins, while watching
Ipswich Town come undone.
He'd show us crowds and corn fields:
immaculate rows of purl stitch, binding off
with stories of Captain Scott knitting
his way through the Antarctic winter.
In the evenings he reminisced
about old episodes of *Knit with Norbury*.
He carried his crochet hook like a penknife;
would think nothing of leaving the office
to fix a dropped stitch; he gave us
a copy each of *The Manly Art of Knitting*.
In summer, we threw ourselves into the surf
diving through loops of brown waves.
When we were bullied, he told us to think
about the big centre forward who knitted
the world's longest football scarf. That summer
he led us to Normandy, threw open the doors
to the great hall at Bayeux and cried:
'This, is this what you call women's work?'

Christopher James

Janet's

Cancelling the wool order
for Mum's unfinished cardigan
was the last time I entered Janet's –
a hushed world where voices spoke of
the 'op' and the 'things they didn't let him know'.
Janet's voice was thickly cabled,
sentences slowly unravelling
as she fetched from the back wools 'put by'.
Rowan, Fair Isle, Mohair, 4 ply
collected weekly
crinkling in expanding cellophane.

Anchor embroidery silks, shell buttons
glowed in that treasure house.
Twirling stands of surgical bits:
fasteners, zippers, hooks and eyes,
row counters and knitting needle weaponry
waited primed.

In the pattern room knitters flicked
through strange family albums: children
knelt awkwardly, always smiling,
women's shoulders at jaunty angles,
real men, rugged and purposeful.

Knit one purl one.
the key to the kingdom.

Sue Dymoke

The Knitting Song

Soldier lad, on the sodden ground,
Sailor lad on the seas,
Can't you hear a little clicketty sound
Stealing across on the breeze?
It's the knitting-needles singing their song
As they twine the khaki or blue,
Thousands and thousands and thousands strong,
Tommy and Jack, for you.

Click — click — click,
How they dart and flick,
Flashing in the firelight to and fro!
Now for purl and plain,
Round and round again,
Knitting love and luck in every row.

The busy hands may be rough or white,
The fingers gouty or slim,
The careful eyes may be youthfully bright,
Or they may be weary and dim,
Lady and workgirl, young and old,
They've all got one end in view,
Knitting warm comforts against the cold,
Tommy and Jack, for you.

Knitting away by the midnight oil,
Knitting when day begins,
Lads, in the stress of your splendid toil,
Can't you hear the song of the pins?
Clicketty, click — through the wind and the foam
It's telling the boys over there
That every "woolly" that comes from home
Brings a smile and a hope and a prayer.

> Click — click — click,
> How they dart and flick,
> Flashing in the firelight to and fro!
> Now for purl and plain,
> Round and round again,
> Knitting love and luck in every row.

Jessie Pope (1868 – 1941)

Wool

Our knitting
is the length of a motorway
                    the distance
        from a landed plane
                to its long haul destination
            the journey that the light makes
in the morning   from the sun.

We've been knitting   for a long time.
We didn't notice

                    when our tension lessened
not at first   but then -
                our needles

kept on missing.

We were knitting
                    but we kept on
        dropping
                off each other's stitches

we couldn't feel each other's fingers
            moving in the dark.

It happened gradually
               loop by purl
      slip by start
but kept on
                until the last

till our knitting lay undone

and all our wool

lay dense

between us.

Lydia Towsey

Dropped Stitches

I start again, I start again.
The chill is going from my hands as I knit,
counting. I tug away the top rows carefully

to get rid of the last mistakes.
They float off somewhere historical
or hierarchical, these light, gone, telegraphic places

that I make with my own two hands:
what I give away, not knowing
how it happened, how I did it.

Jane Duran

Needle Work

She pierces yarn with needles,
sets aside four inches of garter stitch,
walks into the hall where he's fallen,
the worse for bitter and the best of a bottle
of rum, his feet still out on the step,
door open to the frivolity of moths.

She puts a shilling in the slot,
lets last night's supper slow-burn
on the stove again, pulls on her coat,
pauses at the mirror to set her hat,
to slip on gloves, before going to see
the woman who unpicks problems.

Back again she checks his pockets
for the inch of chalk he used to spy,
feels him suck her breath through his teeth,
re-marks the soles of her shoes,
resumes her knitting, picks up the stitch
she'd dropped and waits.

Allison McVety

Neighbours We'll Not Part Tonight

Roll me round to the stories of the great knittings
That took place in the foretimes
About the woollen northern country
In a smell of straw and peat and smoky kitchens;

    With a 'clack!' for a sound
    We're knitting the houses round

As the great sheep's eye of the sun slunk down behind the fell
And his thick grey blanket folded its long rows over
Door after door closed soft as the mighty strode,
Staggered, ran, limped, in the dark to their knitting spell;

    With a step for a sound
    We're knitting the houses round

There was Ram's-Back Rachel, Black Tick and Tam Tup,
Six-Pin Tirleyman (Twistaway Gannelbone's grandson)
Little Stichy Baby and Kitty Curl, Granny Pullock with the
                               straddle legs,
And a long pale idiot man who would knit with his toes:
                              these made the party up;

    With a breath for a sound
    We're knitting the houses round

Then came the girls Pocket and Flitty, and Ribber Wagstaff
                          with his strong thumbs,
Giantess Appleyard in ten petticoats and not perspiring,
And Schoolmaster Weazell with his knitted walking stick,
Come to set all the children their knitting sums.

    With a squeeze for a sound
    We're knitting the houses round

Where was the clicking of laughter then but amid the smoke
When the knitting songs and the knitting stories ran free,
And the mutton-grease fumbled the wool,
And the wool-swaddled babes in the loft began to choke?

   With a laugh for a sound
   We're knitting the houses round

When it's long past midnight and the yards of knitting enfold
Foot upon stamping foot, not gingerly pressed together,
And the flushed pink faces still mouth out the rows of song
Then the joy of the knitting runs stitches through young and old;

   With a gasp for a sound
   We're knitting the houses round

Then the needles fly faster and faster; wondrous rows fall
Like foam in the beck from the warm long-labouring fingers;
Pile on the floor, to the last knitting hymn, round knees,
                            waists, bosoms, and envelope
All the great passionate ones in a soft breathing pall;

   With a tactful silence
   We're knitting the houses round

Roy Fisher

For My Grandmother Knitting

There is no need they say
but the needles still move
their rhythms in the working of your hands
as easily
as if your hands
were once again those sure and skillful hands
of the fisher-girl.

You are old now
and your grasp of things is not so good
but master of your moments then
deft and swift
you slit the still-ticking quick silver fish.
Hard work it was too
of necessity.

But now they say there is no need
as the needles move
in the working of your hands
once the hands of the bride
with the hand-span waist
once the hands of the miner's wife
who scrubbed his back
in a tin bath by the coal fire
once the hands of the mother
of six who made do and mended
scraped and slaved slapped sometimes
when necessary.

But now they say there is no need
the kids they say grandma
have too much already
more than they can wear
too many scarves and cardigans –
gran you do too much
there's no necessity.
At your window you wave
them goodbye Sunday.
With your painful hands
big on shrunken wrists.
Swollen-jointed. Red. Arthritic. Old.
But the needles still move
their rhythms in the working of your hands
easily
as if your hands remembered
of their own accord the pattern
as if your hands had forgotten
how to stop.

Liz Lochhead

Untitled

Autumn – overlooked my Knitting –
Dyes – said He – have I –
Could disparage a Flamingo –
Show Me them – said I –

Cochineal – I chose – for deeming
It resemble Thee –
And the little Border – Dusker –
For resembling Me –

Emily Dickinson (1830 – 1886)

'I thanke God, and ever shall,
It is the sheepe hath payed for all.'

Inscribed in a house of a Merchant of the Staple